Round Table Series 56

The many faces of depression

D1808491

Edited by

Malcolm Lader and

Alan Wade

Proceedings of a Round Table discussion held at the
Royal Society of Medicine, London, on 3 February 1999.
These discussions reflect the experience and opinions of
the panellists and do not necessarily reflect the opinions of
the Royal Society of Medicine nor the recommendations of
SmithKline Beecham.

Published by the Royal Society of Medicine Press Ltd with
financial support from SmithKline Beecham.

The ROYAL
SOCIETY *of*
MEDICINE
PRESS *Limited*

These proceedings are published by the Royal Society of Medicine Press
Ltd with financial support from the sponsor. The contributors are
responsible for the scientific content and for the views expressed, which
are not necessarily those of the sponsor, of the editor of the series or of
the volume, of the Royal Society of Medicine or of the Royal Society of
Medicine Press Ltd. Distribution has been in accordance with the wishes
of the sponsors but a copy is available to any fellow of the Society at a
privileged price.

British Library Cataloguing in Publication Data

A catalogue record for this book is available from the British Library

ISBN 1-85315-417-2
ISSN 0268-3091

Typeset by Dobbie Typesetting Limited, Tavistock, Devon
Printed in Great Britain by Finesse Print, Maidstone, Kent

Participants

CHAIR

Professor Malcolm Lader

Professor of Clinical Psychopharmacology, Institute of Psychiatry, University of London, De Crespigny Park, Denmark Hill, London SE5 8AF

PARTICIPANTS

Dr Tim Bullock

Consultant Psychiatrist, West London Healthcare NHS Trust, Uxbridge Road, Southall, Middlesex UB1 3EU

Dr Martin Deahl

Consultant and Senior Lecturer in Psychiatric Medicine, Homerton Hospital NHS Trust, Homerton Row, Hackney, London E9 6SR

Mr John Donoghue

Independent Pharmacy Consultant, 4 Wrenfield Grove, Liverpool LI7 9QD

Dr Chris Manning

General Practitioner, 95 Langham Road, Teddington, Middlesex TWII 9HG

Dr Richard Maxwell

General Practitioner, Terra Firma, 15 York Gardens, Clifton, Bristol BS8 4LL

Professor Jan Scott

Professor of Community Psychiatry, Department of Psychiatry, University of Newcastle, Royal Victoria Infirmary, Newcastle Upon Tyne NEI 4LP

Dr Alan Wade

General Practitioner, Clydebank Health Centre, Kilbowie Road, Clydebank, Dunbarton G81 7TQ

Contents

Introduction

Malcolm Lader

Depression is a complex disease consisting of many overlapping conditions. It has many faces and patients present to their doctor in different ways. The many faces of depression are often masked, making diagnosis difficult in the primary care setting. Therefore, there is concern that the recognition and treatment of depression in primary care is not ideal, and ways of improving it need to be found.

The main purpose of this meeting was to raise awareness about the complexity of depression among GPs. This is particularly important in the context of unusual presentations, such as those occurring in certain age groups, which are often missed during the short time available at a consultation. Treatment options are discussed with a view to matching the therapy to the particular presentation(s) so that the patient achieves the best outcome.

What constitutes depression and what is the evidence?

Malcolm Lader

In 1621, Robert Burton wrote in his *Anatomy of Melancholy*, "I say of our melancholy man, he is the cream of human adversity, the quintessence and upshot; all other disease whatsoever are flea-bitings to melancholy in extent: 'tis the pith of them all". The term 'melancholy' was used to describe depression for the next 300 years. Today, psychiatrists use the symptoms of depressive disorder defined by the International Classification of Diseases (ICD-10) [1] and the Diagnostic and Statistical Manual, fourth edition (DSM-IV) [2] to aid in diagnosis (Table 1). A certain number and type of symptoms need to be present to diagnose a patient with major or minor depression.

The diagnosis of patients referred to secondary care is usually clear because of the severity, duration and characteristics of the symptoms; however, depression is less easy to diagnose in general practice. Although loss of interest can be quantified on questioning (eg does the patient still enjoy playing golf or seeing their grand-children?) and fatigue and decreased energy can be commonly described, features such as depressed mood or diminished concentration are less easily recognized.

Depression in the primary care setting is a complex of overlapping symptoms, often camouflaged to the point of obscurity. The symptoms range from agitation to

TABLE 1   Symptoms of depressive disorder in ICD-10 and DSM-IV [1, 2]

1.	Depressed mood for two weeks
2.	Loss of interest
3.	Fatigue or decreased energy
4.	Loss of confidence or self-esteem
5.	Self-reproach or guilt
6.	Recurrent thoughts of death, suicide or suicidal behaviour
7.	Diminished concentration or indecisiveness
8.	Agitation or retardation
9.	Sleep disturbance (insomnia or hypersomnia)
10.	Appetite and weight change (increase or decrease)

DSM-IV, major depression: five symptoms including 1 or 2 (4 not listed)

ICD-10, severe depression: eight symptoms including 1 and 2 or 3

Moderate depression: six symptoms including two of 1, 2 or 3

Mild depression: four symptoms including two of 1 and 2 or 3 stupor, from sleep disturbances to insomnia or polysomnia/hypersomnia and from anorexia to hyperphagia, and have an emphasis ranging from cognitive to somatic. There is a spectrum of anxiety level and intellectual impairment. A depressive co-morbidity is often seen with conditions such as drug abuse or anorexia, and depression can be a releasing mechanism for other forms of behaviour. Agoraphobia, for example, may increase in severity if the sufferer also becomes depressed. Underlying psychiatric conditions can be made worse by depression and come to the GP's notice. Depression is sometimes unmasked when anxiety is treated.

Primary depression can be accompanied by anxiety, melancholia or psychosis (mood congruent or mood incongruent). Many people with anxiety-related disorders go on to develop depression, and the depression makes the condition worse. Some patients become so severely depressed that they lose contact with reality; on investigation it may be discovered that they originally had depression alone, which was followed by the development of anxiety and eventually by psychotic features.

The core symptoms of depression can be listed as a diagnostic scale, containing features relating to diagnosis, and a depression scale, measuring the severity of the depression (Table 2) [2,3].

A number of factors can obscure a diagnosis of depression in general practice. First, the precipitating 'cause' does not obviate the need for treatment. There is a tendency to deal with the cause of the depression rather than treat the disorder in its own right, and causes of depression that appear valid and persuasive may not turn out to be the true ones. Second, it is important to look for the presence of anything more than minimal symptoms. Third, the depression should not be ignored in order to treat anxiety. Fourth, if the diagnosis is clouded by physical symptoms the GP should ask about depression in greater detail. Some patients repeatedly return for consultations with different physical symptoms, and unless this behaviour

TABLE 2 Core symptoms of depression [2,3]

Depression scale (MADRS)	Diagnostic scale (DSM-IV)
Sadness observed or reported inner tension	Depressed mood or irritability
Loss of interest	Loss of interest or pleasure
Reduced appetite	Appetite or weight loss (rarely gain)
Reduced sleep	Sleep loss (or rarely increase)
Concentration difficulty	Diminished concentration
	Psychomotor agitation or retardation
Lassitude	Loss of energy or fatigue
Pessimism	Worthlessness or guilt
Suicidal thoughts	Recurrent suicidal thoughts or thoughts of death

is considered in more detail the diagnosis will be missed, resulting in needless time-consuming and costly investigations. Worsening of physical symptoms (eg recurring headaches or back trouble) may be due to a 'releasing' effect of the depression.

Depression was reported in about 15% of women and half this number of men in a study of psychiatric symptoms stratified by age and sex. Fatigue was the most common symptom found (35% of women, 10% of men), followed by sleep problems, irritability and worry. Anxiety symptoms were evident, and it is easy to see how they could result in the obfuscation of depression [4].

The US National Co-morbidity Survey, which was carried out in 1990–92 and recruited 8,098 patients aged between 15 and 54 years, found a high co-morbidity of lifetime major depressive disorder with many other psychiatric disorders, particularly agoraphobia, social phobia and substance abuse/alcohol use disorder (Figure 1) [5]. That is, the analysis showed that patients with a lifetime major depressive disorder had previously experienced other psychiatric conditions. Substance abuse is increasing in prevalence and is now seen in almost all the major psychiatric conditions. This in itself results in complications, including the refractory nature of (ie partial or no response to) antidepressant treatment.

Depression is also associated with a number of physical conditions, particularly stroke and cancer (Table 3). Organic depression should also be considered during diagnosis. It has several possible causes: occult carcinoma (lung and pancreas); metabolic and endocrine disorders (hyperthyroidism, hypercalcaemia, Cushing's disease and vitamin B_{12} deficiency); the use of certain drugs (eg steroids, β-blockers, methyldopa, clonidine, nifedipine, digoxin, L-dopa and tetrabenazine); infections (such as post-viral infections, myalgic encephalomyelitis, brucellosis and neurosyphilis); and organic brain disease (space-occupying lesions and dementia).

Depression is common in later life, occurring in 15% of people aged more than 65 years and in 30% of elderly patients who visit their GP. However, it can often be missed and GPs need to look out for it. A misconception is that people who have never suffered from depression are 'immune' to it in later life; in fact, the likelihood of having a first depressive episode increases with age. Depression is often hard to detect in elderly people, and is common in dementia.

Risk factors for developing depression in later life include a previous and family history of the disease, poor health (eg stroke, myocardial infarction, arthritis and bronchitis), widowerhood, personality problems, isolation and lack of confidence. Precipitating factors include the loss of a partner and the effect of certain medications. Important indicators to the physician that an old person is depressed include recent changes in health, circumstances (such as giving up the family home) and consulting behaviour. The GP should watch out for patients who suddenly become regular visitors to the surgery when they normally see their GP once every 10 years.

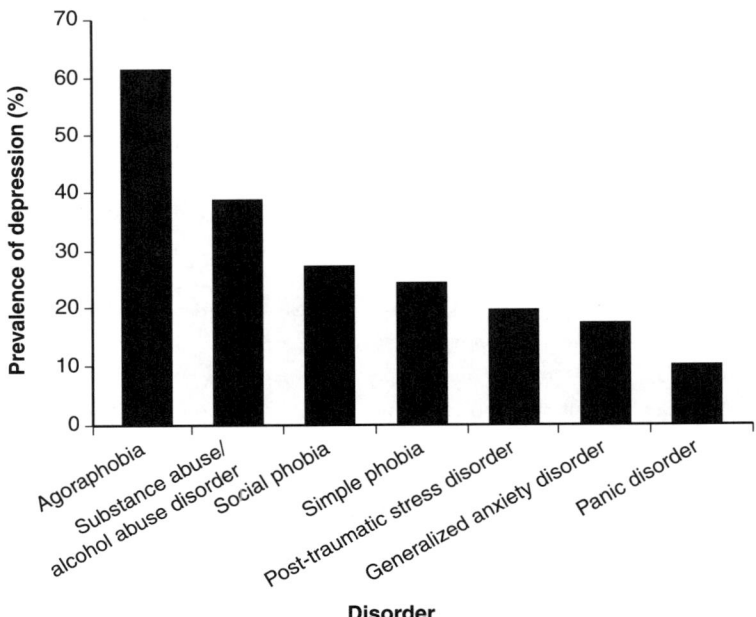

FIGURE I   Co-morbidity of lifetime major depressive disorder with other psychiatric conditions in the US National Co-morbidity Survey. Redrawn and reproduced with permission [5]

In the differential diagnosis of depressive pseudodementia from primary dementia several factors must be considered. Depressive pseudodementia has an acute onset, past affective episodes are common, there is self-reproach, it is worse in the morning and memory, overall, is affected. Primary dementia, however, is insidious, is not characterized by affective episodes or self-reproach, is worse at night and produces memory deficit with respect to recent events. Where differential diagnosis

TABLE 3   Prevalence rates of depression with physical disorders

Disorder	Prevalence of depression (%)
Stroke	22–60
Myocardial infarction	35–45
Cancer	42
Parkinson's disease	40
Rheumatoid arthritis	21
Irritable bowel syndrome	21
Diabetes	14–18
Chronic obstructive airways disease	16

is difficult, the trial of an antidepressant is justified. Pseudodemented patients react to failure by giving up but can be coached, while those with primary dementia may have a catastrophic reaction with consistently poor results on coaching.

Old people do not usually report their mood and are ashamed of being depressed, preferring to stress bodily symptoms. Furthermore, some doctors are wary of prescribing antidepressants to older people because of concerns over intolerance. The suicide rate generally increases with age, bereavement, isolation, deteriorating health and pain. Actual and attempted suicide are closely linked, and the psychiatrist should be involved in cases of known suicide risk.

Dysthymia is a chronic, mild form of depression. To be diagnosed with dysthymia, according to DSM-IV criteria [2], the patient must present with depressed mood for most of the day and for more days than not for at least two years (A). While depressed they need to exhibit at least two of the following characteristics: poor appetite, insomnia or hypersomnia, low energy or fatigue and low self-esteem, poor concentration or difficulty making decisions (B). During a two-year period of the disturbance they should never be without the symptoms in A or B for more than two months at a time. Dysthymia probably merges into major depressive disorder but is diagnosed on the basis of the duration and severity of the depression. In reality it may be chronic depression that has been exacerbated. The DSM-IV criteria also state that the patient must present with no evidence of an unequivocal major depressive episode during the first two years of the disturbance. To be considered dysthymic, patients must never have had a manic episode or unequivocal hypomanic episode, or one superimposed on a chronic psychotic disorder (eg schizophrenia). It must be established that no organic factor could have initiated and maintained the disturbance (such as prolonged administration of antihypertensive medication), and the symptoms must cause the patient clinically significant distress or impairment.

Brief recurrent depressive disorder is another presentation of depression. It is described as follows by the American Psychiatry Association (APA) 1994 criteria [2]. Criteria for a depressive episode must be met, with depressive periods lasting for at least two days and less than two weeks. The periods must occur at least twice a month for 12 consecutive months and not be associated with the menstrual cycle. They must cause significant distress to the patient and not be due to substance abuse or a medical condition. Brief recurrent depressive disorder is difficult to treat as the disease is often in remission by the time an antidepressant has had time to work.

Anxiety and depressive states have a number of different features that can be used to aid diagnosis (Table 4). Depression is characterized by loss of libido, sleep and appetite. Patients with depressive tension may lose weight without much change in appetite. Depression may also present as a sleep disorder. Patients often fall asleep quickly, but characteristically awaken frequently during the night and finally wake up early. Ford and Kamerow studied insomnia and depression in the

TABLE 4   Cross-sectional features differentiating anxiety and depressive states

Anxiety	Depression
Hypervigilance	Psychomotor retardation
Severe tension and panic	Severe sadness
Perceived danger	Perceived loss
Phobic avoidance	Loss of interest — anhedonia
Doubt and uncertainty	Hopelessness (suicidal)
Insecurity	Self-deprecation
Performance anxiety	Loss of libido
	Early morning awakening
	Weight loss

primary care setting, carrying out two interviews 12 months apart [6]. Overall, at either interview, about 10% of the attendees complained of insomnia. If there was no insomnia at either interview the incidence of depression was low (0.4%) during the year between the two interviews and that of anxiety was only 4.2%. When insomnia was present at the first interview only, the incidence of depression remained similar (0.6%) but the number of patients with anxiety increased to 7.4%. Patients who developed insomnia between the first and second interviews had a greatly increased risk of having depression (a rise from 0.6% to 11.9%), but the incidence of anxiety only rose from 7.4% to 11.0%. The percentage of patients with insomnia at both interviews who were depressed was similar to that of those who had depression at the second interview only (14.0%), while 25.6% of patients had anxiety at both interviews. From these data it was concluded that anxiety is concomitant with insomnia but that depression is likely to have occurred if insomnia developed, indicating that newly presenting insomnia is a marker for depression. GPs confronted by a patient who has recently developed insomnia with no obvious cause (eg jet lag) should therefore consider a primary diagnosis of depression.

In conclusion, depression embraces a series of complex conditions presenting with 'many faces'. It can exist independently, but is often secondary to or co-morbid with other conditions and is common in all physical illness. The complexity and many faces of depression may hinder the recognition of depression in general practice.

Summary

- Depression embraces a series of complex overlapping conditions presenting with 'many faces', making it difficult to diagnose in primary care.

- Depression can exist alone but is often secondary to or co-morbid with many other conditions, including agoraphobia, social phobia, substance abuse/alcohol use disorder, obsessive–compulsive disorder, panic attacks and anxiety.
- Depression is common in all physical illness, particularly stroke, cancer and Parkinson's disease.
- Depression may have an organic cause, such as occult carcinoma, metabolic and endocrine disorders, the use of certain drugs, infections and organic brain disease.
- The diagnosis of depression may be obscured by precipitating 'causes', anxiety and physical symptoms.
- Depression is common in later life and may be hard to diagnose in elderly patients — important indicators to the physician that an elderly person is depressed include recent changes in health, circumstances and consulting behaviour.
- Depression can be characterized by loss of libido, sleep and appetite. Newly pre-senting insomnia with no obvious cause is a marker for depression.
- Consider dysthymia and brief recurrent depressive disorder in patients present-ing with symptoms of depression.
- A number of scores and scales are available to help GPs determine the severity of depression.

References

1   *International Statistical Classification of Disease and Related Health Problems*, 10th ed. Geneva: WHO, 1992.

2   *Diagnostic Criteria from DSM-IV and Statistical Manual of Mental Disorders*, 4th ed. Washington DC: American Psychiatric Association, 1994.

3   Montgomery SA, Asberg M. A new depression scale designed to be sensitive to change. *Br J Psychiatry* 1979; **134**: 382–9.

4   Bebbington PE, Dunn G, Jenkins R *et al*. The influence of age and sex on the prevalence of depressive conditions: report from the National Survey of Psychiatric Morbidity. *Psychol Med* 1998; **28**(1): 9–19.

5   Kessler RC, Nelson CB, McGonagle J *et al*. Comorbidity of DSM-III-R major depressive disorder in the general population: results from the US National Comorbidity Survey. *Br J Psychiatry* 1996; **168**(30): 7–30.

6   Ford DE, Kamerow DB. Epidemiologic study of sleep disturbances and psychiatric disorders. An opportunity for prevention. *JAMA* 1989; **262**(11): 1479–84.

Diagnosis in primary care

Alan Wade

Probably fewer than 50% of all depressed patients visit their GP, depression is diagnosed in less than half of these and a smaller number still receive treatment. Antidepressant therapy, when it is initiated at all, is inadequate in many cases, primarily due to the prescribing of low doses of tricyclic antidepressants. This has led to claims that the outcome at one year is the same in primary care, whether a patient with depression is treated or not [1]. The combination of underpresentation by the patient, underdiagnosis by the GP and undertreatment results in a poor outcome for people with depression.

Patients fail to present to their doctor for several reasons. A stigma is still associated with depression in people of all ages. Elderly people and their relatives tend to accept depression as a natural part of being old, relating it to factors such as bereavement and declining health. Depression, however, is often first recognized by relatives, who see a change in the patient's behaviour and insist on a visit to the GP. Even when depression is recognized, patients have poor expectations of the treatment on offer and may make a conscious decision not to attend. The solution to these problems will involve education, for example through patient support groups and a public health campaign that not only educates about recognition but also promotes the value of treatment. According to a MORI poll, the Defeat Depression Campaign has had some impact on attitudes, increasing public acceptance that depression is a medical condition that anyone can suffer from and that it should be treated with antidepressants. Interestingly, although the people surveyed generally thought GPs were well trained, they also believed these doctors were likely to be unsympathetic. Such opinions will not encourage people with depression to visit their GP.

GPs behaviour in diagnosing depression has been investigated [2]. GPs were asked to rank, in order of importance: general impression as an individual enters their consulting room; the symptoms described (eg losing sleep); any observed signs (ie body language); ability to function. A general combination of all four ranked highest. The likelihood of eliciting a variety of signs and symptoms was then determined. Asking about symptoms, for example sleeplessness, was ranked high but function-related factors, such as ability to handle money, was ranked low. It appears that, although GPs consider functional behavioural changes important, they do not ask about them during consultation. A greater emphasis on functionality may be an important aspect of GP education.

According to Tylee *et al*, if a patient 'describes a more distinct quality to their depressed mood' — in other words, presents with a psychological, rather than a physical, symptom — depression is more likely to be diagnosed [3]. However, most patients present with oblique and non-specific indications of depression such as tiredness and physical illness, which often go unrecognized. In the World Health Organization (WHO) Primary Care Study, the investigators obtained a diagnosis from the GP and then gave patients a Composite International Diagnostic Interview questionnaire from which to establish a true psychiatric diagnosis [4]. The questionnaire detected an incidence of depression of 10%. Although GPs recognized most of these cases as having a psychological basis, they identified only a small proportion of them as 'depression', and in many cases diagnosed anxiety or mixed anxiety and depression in these individuals (Figure 1).

Groups at particular risk of developing depression are elderly people, individuals with co-morbid physical illnesses and those who have suffered bereavement or redundancy. When 500 UK GPs and 250 GPs from Denmark were asked to provide the age and gender of their most recently treated depressed patient, it materialized that few patients over the age of 60 were being treated (Figure 2) [5]. Why should

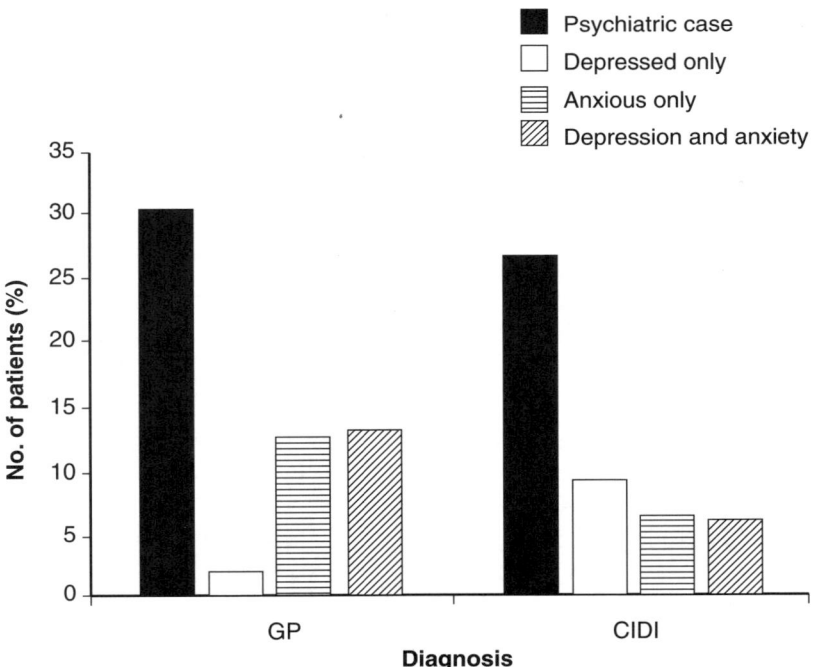

FIGURE 1 World Health Organization Primary Care Study: diagnosis by GP and Composite International Diagnostic Interview questionnaire [4]

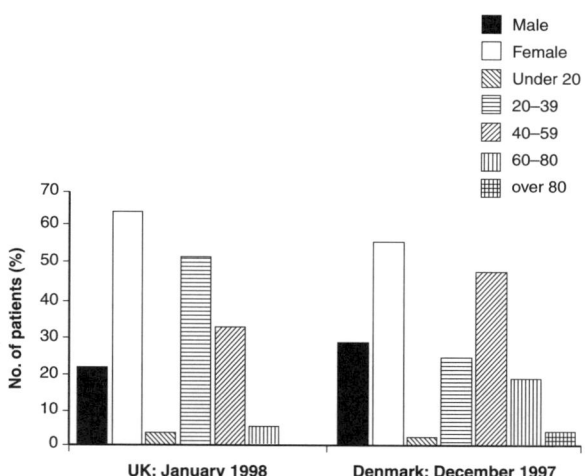

FIGURE 2 Age and gender of the most recently treated depressed patients in the UK (January 1998) and Denmark (December 1997) [5]

this be? Depression in elderly people has a different presentation from that in younger people. Older patients most commonly present with somatic symptoms, anxiety, aggression, sleep disturbance and motivational disturbance or agitation. Many, feeling that psychological symptoms are socially unacceptable, sublimate the latter into physical symptoms. Anxiety is the most common psychological symptom and depression is often hidden by co-morbid anxiety. Depression is also frequently underdiagnosed in people with co-morbid physical illness. It is difficult for GPs to identify depression in people who have cancer or whose partner has died, for example, as it is 'natural' to be anxious under such circumstances.

GPs, therefore, bias their diagnosis towards their impression, which is usually one of an anxiety disorder. This is particularly true of at-risk groups.

Although depression scales are perceived as useful aids to diagnosis and their administration can be delegated to other members of the practice team, for

TABLE 1 Practical advice for GPs

- Be aware of at-risk groups
- Be aware that anxiety symptoms are a common component of depression
- Remember that depression is a long-term illness, like hypertension, and can last for a lifetime
- Time management in the surgery may be of value
- There is a need for a public health campaign (although the Defeat Depression Campaign has had little impact)

example the practice nurse, most GPs do not use them. A survey of 468 UK GPs in early 1998 established that 1.3% always used scales, 3.6% often used them, 16.0% occasionally used them and the majority, 79%, did not use them at all [2]. The Hamilton Depression Scale was applied most frequently (by 31% of those who used a scale), while the Edinburgh Postnatal Depression Scale (EPNDS) was applied most consistently (in 21%). The wide use of the EPNDS may be the result of its recent adoption by the Royal College of Midwives. Most (89%) people who used the EPNDS were female. The people actually using the scales were not identified in the survey, so they may have been midwives carrying out routine postnatal checks or health visitors rather than GPs. Although the simplification of a scale is thought to encourage its use, reduction of the geriatric depression scale to four questions has had no impact on uptake. Of the GPs using scales in the survey, 35% were female and only 15% were male [2]. This may be because female GPs see more cases of postnatal depression than their male colleagues, but there is some indication that age is a factor: 27% of doctors qualified for under 15 years used scales compared with 19% of those qualified for 15 years or more.

GPs work about 60 hours a week, and many people believe they have insufficient time to see individual patients. A questionnaire perception study completed by 210 GPs found that the participants thought they saw an average of 26 depressed patients each week [6]. In addition, 95% of the GPs thought people with depression took up more time than the average patient, 80% estimated that initial appointments with depressed patients lasted for 11–30 min and more than half thought that more than 40% of the depressed patients were somatizing. Thus, GPs feel they take more time seeing and diagnosing patients with depression than people with other conditions, particularly if somatizing takes place. The top three time-consuming activities reported by the GPs were somatizing—trying to work out non-existent physical symptoms before settling on a diagnosis of depression (65%), counselling—time taken to do this (59%), and establishing rapport with the patient—time taken to gain trust (37%).

As part of an in-depth diary study, four GPs wrote down everything they did every 10 min during a week [6]. Surprisingly, depression consultations comprised only 3% of the consultation time and took an average of eight minutes each. The doctors spent most time dealing with musculo-skeletal disorders, followed by gastrointestinal upsets.

There is, therefore, a gap between reality and perception. GPs say they see many depressed patients, but may, in fact, not be diagnosing depression they 'know' is there and be 'colluding' with somatized depression instead. It may be easier and quicker to prescribe painkillers for a depressed patient somatizing with backache than to look for the underlying problem they sub-consciously 'know' is there. This may have short-term time-saving benefits for the individual GP, but is likely to result in time-wasting repeat appointments in the long term, as well as a delay in treatment onset for the patient. Improving the diagnosis and management of depression would have important time-saving implications.

The Royal College of General Practitioners/Royal College of Physicians joint statement, which mimics the WHO statement on recommended treatment lengths, recommends that patients with depression should be treated for four to six months post-symptom resolution. Although many GPs agree with this statement only 20% strongly agree. Even these are unlikely to have or take the extra time to encourage patient compliance. Compliance is a major problem in depression, and the average length of treatment in the UK is only 6–9 weeks [7]. Many patients do not receive an adequate number of repeat prescriptions, and "Too often a prescription signals the end of an interview rather than the start of an alliance" [8].

Summary

- Depression is underpresented by patients (ie, they sublimate it during consultation), under-recognized by GPs and undertreated, leading to poor outcome.
- Treatment is often inadequate in patients who receive it, and the duration of antidepressant therapy averages only 6–9 weeks in the UK, lower than the guidelines stated by WHO.
- Depressed patients fail to present to their doctor because of perceived stigma, acceptance of depression (in older people), poor expectations of treatment and the belief that their GP is unsympathetic. Instead they present with physical illness.
- Although the Defeat Depression Campaign has had some impact on attitudes regarding depression, more public education is needed in the form of further campaigns and patient support groups.
- GPs diagnose primarily by impression, and the impression is usually one of an anxiety disorder. They rarely consider the importance of functional behavioural changes as indications of depression.
- GPs are usually able to recognize psychiatric cases but often misdiagnose depression as anxiety or mixed anxiety and depression.
- Groups at particular risk of developing depression are elderly people, individuals with co-morbid physical illnesses and those who have suffered bereavement or redundancy.
- Depression scales are seldom employed to aid diagnosis although their use can be delegated to another member of the practice staff.
- The lack of time available in a GP-patient consultation can result in the treatment of physical symptoms in somatizing depressed patients rather than the underlying problem.
- Undiagnosed and unmanaged depression has important time implications.

References

1   Goldberg D, Privett M, Ustun B et al. The effects of detection and treatment on the outcome of major depression in primary care: a naturalistic study in 15 cities. Br J Gen Pract 1998; **48**(437): 1840–4.

2   Wade AG. Symptomatic recovery in depression: how much of a cure? XXIst CINP Congress, 1998.

3   Tylee AT, Freeling P, Kerry S. Why do general practitioners recognize major depression in one woman patient yet miss it in another? Br J Gen Pract 1993; **43**(373): 327–30.

4   Ustun T, Sartorius N. Mental illness in general health care. Chichester: John Wiley, 1995.

5   GP exchange meeting on the treatment of depression, Paris, March 1998.

6   Wade AG. Treating Panic and Depression in Primary Care. 11th ECNP Congress, 1998.

7   Paykel ES, Priest RG. Recognition and management of depression in general practice: consensus statement. BMJ 1992; **305**(6863): 1198–202.

8   Blackwell B. Drug therapy: patient compliance. N Engl J Med 1973; **289**(5): 249–52.

Discussion consensus: improving awareness in general practice

Malcolm Lader

- Depression is a complex condition with many manifestations, making it difficult to diagnose in primary care.
- Depression presents in a number of different ways and can be hidden. It is important to search for depression underlying other conditions, such as anxiety and physical symptoms such as insomnia.
- Depressed patients often fail to present to their doctor and depression is under-recognized by GPs. It is therefore undertreated and outcome poor.
- The need for long-term treatment in many cases can lead to poor compliance and impact negatively on outcome.
- Consultation time is limited, so it is important to understand and be aware of the complexity of the condition when making a diagnosis and consider functional and behavioural signs of change as well as physical symptoms.
- Making the diagnosis and initiating appropriate treatment, whether or not the cause of the disease is apparent, will result in a saving of time, distress and handicap.

What are our treatment options?

Jan Scott

The aims of treatment in depression are to reduce symptoms, restore functioning and prevent recurrence and relapse. Treatment can be considered as having acute, continuation and maintenance phases (Figure 1), corresponding to making people well, keeping them well and preventing a return of the disorder.

The treatment options in depression—medication, psychotherapy, combined medication and psychotherapy, and electroconvulsive therapy—work in different ways. Psychological therapies are the only treatments that directly influence symptoms and level of functioning, and prevent recurrence (by changing the patient's coping skills). Drugs have a direct effect on acute symptoms and reduce the risk of recurrence if medication is maintained, but only have an indirect effect on functioning. Drugs do not change how people cope with problems, but they can play an important role. For example, medication will improve the symptoms in a patient with severe depression. This will enable the person to think more clearly and provide a 'window of opportunity' in which they can look at their other problems. Some people have the skills to resolve these problems alone while others need additional input, such as psychological therapies.

The message that effective treatments are available for depression needs to reach primary care. In fact, the success rate in treating depression is as good as that in many other disease areas. In terms of acute response to treatment, the efficacy of antidepressant therapy is more than 60% for major depression, 60% for obsessive–compulsive disorder, 80% for panic and bipolar disorders and 60% for schizophrenia [1]. This compares with 40% for angioplasty and just above 50% for

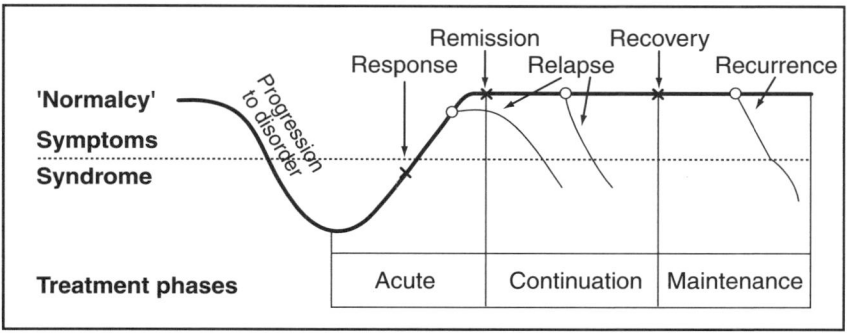

FIGURE 1   Phases of treatment

atherectomy [I]. When patients adhere to medication the same is true of maintenance treatment. Active treatment for major depression has a success rate (in terms of relapse prevention at one year) of 82% compared with 35% for placebo [2]. The corresponding rate for hypertension treatment is 48% versus 25% for placebo. The average acute response rate to antidepressants in day-to-day clinical practice is 58% [3]. Other individual treatments, such as cognitive therapy, interpersonal therapy and behaviour therapy, have response rates of 50–55% [3]. Acute treatment with short-term, effective psychological therapies therefore has similar effectiveness to antidepressants.

Primary care doctors have a range of treatments to choose from for patients with depression, so how do they decide what is best? For help with choosing medication, peer-reviewed clinical practice guidelines on the treatment of depression can be helpful. In a recent study, the five peer-reviewed guidelines on the treatment of depression in primary care (Agency for Health Care Policy and Research (AHPCR), North of England, *Effective Healthcare Bulletin*, Royal College of Psychiatrists and General Practitioners, and British Association of Psychopharmacology) were assessed using the Institute of Medicine tool designed for such a purpose. However, none of the guidelines scored highly for quality standard and validity [4]. To help GPs, valid, reliable and high-quality guidelines are needed.

As part of the study, a group of GPs was asked which questions they would most like a set of guidelines to answer. They wanted to know the threshold at which to start treatment, which drug should be used as first-line treatment, how to assess the effectiveness of the treatment, information on issues relating to continuation of therapy, what to do if the first treatment of choice does not work, when to try psychological therapies and when to try a different drug. None of the current peer-reviewed guidelines answered all of these basic questions.

Once medication has been prescribed, the next problem is how to ensure patients actually adhere with treatment. This is a major problem, as 50% of patients prescribed an antidepressant stop taking it within six weeks and 10% do not even take the prescription to the chemists (primary non-adherence) [4]. Adherence was studied in the US by Lin *et al*, who attempted to identify which aspects of the patient, the doctor–patient relationship and the treatment (eg side-effects) might be involved and the educational messages needed to encourage people to take medication [5]. Of the 155 patients in the study, 28% stopped taking the antidepressants within a month and 44% by the third month. Although severe side-effects had some impact, it was found that patients were most likely to stay on the medication if they had been given clear messages about what to expect. Adherence was greater in the first month if the following specific messages were given:

- take the antidepressant daily
- the drug must be taken for 2–4 weeks for a benefit to be seen

- continue taking the medication even if you feel better
- do not stop taking it without consulting your doctor.

Instructions were also given on how to resolve specific problems, for example what to do about missed doses.

Katon *et al* put these messages into practice, working with primary care physicians [6]. These researchers randomly allocated 217 patients diagnosed with major or minor depression into two groups. Patients in group 1 were given 'normal' care and those in group 2 received 'multi-faceted intervention', involving the use of educational and video materials, meetings with a consultant psychiatrist, surveillance of antidepressant medication refills and some monitoring of adherence. For patients with major depression, significant differences in adherence were found between groups 1 and 2 (50% versus 75%, respectively, $p < 0.01$). For minor depression there was also a significant difference, with adherence of 40% in group 1 and 80% in group 2 ($p < 0.01$). This increase in adherence resulted in a more favourable outcome for the patients with major depression but not for those with minor depression. However, all individuals who received the multi-faceted intervention reported improved satisfaction with care, and the treatment was well accepted.

Every intervention has a psychological component, even the GP writing the prescription and educating a patient about their disorder. However, the most effective psychological therapies (brief dynamic therapy, interpersonal therapy and cognitive behavioural therapy) share certain characteristics that distinguish them from ineffective ones. They have a coherent theoretical model and a flexibly applied, structured approach with logical sequential interventions based on a formulation for the particular patient. They also emphasize skills development, the independent use of those skills and, importantly, attribute change to the patient [7]. Brief dynamic therapy is used fairly often clinically but has not been the subject of much research. Interpersonal therapy is popular in the US and has performed well in research trials, but there are few clinical practitioners in the UK. The effectiveness of cognitive therapy is well supported by research evidence and trained therapists are available, but not enough to cope with demand. Interestingly, counselling does not meet the criteria for an effective therapy. It is helpful in the short term or in a crisis and is liked by both patients and GPs, but does not appear to prevent future relapse of depression or change people's coping styles.

When should psychological therapy be the treatment of choice for depressed patients in primary care? The predictors of non-response to both medication and psychological treatments are: severity, endogenicity, chronicity, double depression, social dysfunction, cognitive dysfunction and expectation of improvement [8]. In acute depression, the response rate to psychological therapies is similar to that obtained with drugs. However, the more severe the depression, the less successful the psychological therapy is likely to be. People with severe depression usually need medication to stabilize their mental state before introducing psychological therapy, and additional therapy sessions will probably be needed. Psychotherapy can work, but t is better to combine it with drugs in such patients.

Although it is difficult to determine the clinical effectiveness of combination therapy from research data, Hollon et al [9] suggest that combination therapy (ie drug plus cognitive therapy) provides an additional 15% improvement in symptom ratings compared with drugs alone. Until people who respond differentially to psychological therapies such as cognitive therapy, or to drugs, can be identified more reliably, choice of treatment will continue to depend on factors such as cost, availability of therapists, or patient and clinician preference.

For many years now, it has been suggested that psychological therapies are too expensive to provide routinely. However, cost-benefit and cost-effectiveness data do not support this assumption, as demonstrated by an acute study in Scotland and a follow-up study in the USA. Researchers in Edinburgh carried out a cost-benefit study of GP treatment versus cognitive therapy versus psychiatric treatment (amitriptyline plus sessions with a psychiatrist) versus brief, dynamic psychotherapy provided by a social worker [10]. When cost of treatment and symptom reduction were compared, there were no significant differences between these treatment options.

Longer-term outcome was studied in four small groups of patients who received treatment for an acute episode of depression and were followed up for two years in the USA [11]. Patients in the first group received medication alone and stopped treatment at four months. Those in the second group received drugs for four months followed by maintenance therapy for two years. The third group was given drugs (both acute and maintenance treatment) plus 16 sessions of cognitive therapy. In all, 50% of the patients who stopped medication relapsed in the two years of follow-up (Figure 2). The relapse rate of those who remained on medication or received cognitive therapy alone or combination therapy was about half that (22–25%) of those who stopped their medication after four months. This is the first study ever to have shown that an antidepressant treatment—namely cognitive therapy—continues to work after it has been stopped. The relapse rates in the cognitive therapy group were similar to those in patients who remained on maintenance medication for two years. This is particularly noteworthy because, in the clinical setting, many patients will stop taking their antidepressants after recovery and therefore be at high risk of relapse. Most importantly, any additional cost of cognitive therapy seems to be offset by the reduced relapse rates and therefore reduced use of health service resources during the follow-up phase.

A more serious drawback to the use of psychological treatments is the lack of access to appropriately trained therapists. The expertise of the therapist is

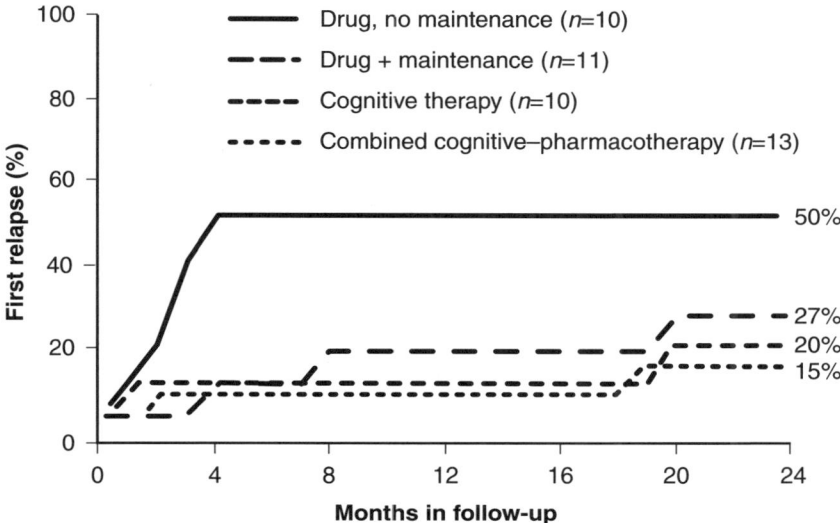

FIGURE 2   Prognosis and long-term outcome in drug therapy and combined therapy: relapse using conservative criteria (two consecutive Beck Depression Inventory scores ⩾16). Redrawn and reproduced with permission [11]

particularly important in complex or severe cases [7]—exactly the types of patient likely to be referred by their GP. Since therapist skill and degree of fidelity to the treatment model accounts for at least 30% variance in patient outcome [7], this issue clearly needs to be addressed.

One approach to the problem might be to try to develop a briefer model of therapy and to train and encourage primary care staff to undertake it. A shortened form of cognitive therapy has been developed specifically for use by GPs. A randomized, controlled trial in which 48 patients with major depression were allocated to either abbreviated cognitive therapy plus usual (drug) treatment or usual treatment alone, has been undertaken [12]. The abbreviated cognitive therapy consisted of six, 30-minute sessions, plus the use of booklets. The recovery rate at seven weeks was 63% for patients receiving abbreviated cognitive therapy and 23% for those on drugs alone ($p < 0.05$). A significantly greater number of patients taking antidepressants alone dropped out of treatment compared with those also receiving abbreviated cognitive therapy ($p < 0.05$). Unfortunately, the study also revealed that it is difficult to deliver cognitive therapy in three hours, even using trained therapists. Thus, in many cases, the length of time spent undergoing psychological therapies is unlikely to be reduced below eight to 10 hours [7].

However, other brief psychological interventions may be developed from cognitive theory. For example, we know that a number of key elements influence whether or not people engage with, and adhere to, treatment: identity (what is it?); cause (what caused it?); timeline (how long will it last?); consequences (how will it/has it affected me?); and cure (can it be controlled or cured?). If a patient's under-standing of this fits with their day-to-day practical experience, and if the GP's suggestions as to how to manage the patient's problems are coherent with the patient's experience and understanding, there is a good chance the treatment will be accepted and adhered to. These are straightforward sensible questions, and most patient support groups actually provide such information. Current work is there-fore investigating whether or not this information can be 'packaged' in a way that is useful to patients without increasing GP workload. It may be possible to develop

TABLE I   Strategic choices in the acute treatment of major depressive disorder (from the AHC^{3}R Guidelines). Treatment phases, objectives and options should be defined with patient (and family where appropriate)

Medication*	Formal psychotherapy	Combined treatment	Electroconvulsive therapy[‡]
More severe	Less severe	More severe	Psychotic
Chronic	Less chronic	Chronic	Severe or extremely severe
Recurrent	Non-psychotic	Partial response to either treatment alone	Prior positive response
Psychotic	Prior positive response	Availability	Failure on several medications or combined treatment trials
Melancholic	Availability	Personality disorder[†]	Need for rapid response
Prior positive response	Medical contraindications to medications	Patient preference	Medical contraindications to medications
Family history	Patient preference**		
Patient preference			
Failure to respond to psychotherapy			

*Medication is always combined with clinical management.

**Patient preference applies more if depression is mild and non-psychotic.

[†]This recommendation has not been empirically tested. It rests solely on clinical experience.

[‡]Electroconvulsive therapy is seldom required for patients seen in primary care settings. It is nearly always reserved for those who have severe, often chronic, often psychotic, depressions that have not responded to several trials of different standard medications.

four or five questions that GPs or clinicians could use to check a patient's understanding in order to maximize adherence.

Strategic choices in the acute treatment of major depression disorder are summarized in Table 1. Patient preference is also important, as a previous positive response to a therapy is a good reason for using it and also correlates significantly with outcome [7]. Symptoms may be alleviated with antidepressants in many cases, but the patient may require another intervention to help them deal with day-to-day problems and to learn a coping style with which to handle future life events. In reality, there is no such treatment as 'drugs alone', since the clinical management of drug treatment always involves a psychological element.

Certain 'add-ons' to clinical management (eg brief cognitive therapy) can be delivered in primary care and simple information, messages and booklets can be used to enhance the impact of drug treatment. At present, drug treatment is the simplest, most widely available approach to the primary care of people with depression, and as much as GPs would like to offer alternatives such as psychological therapy, the latter will still have to be used selectively until more therapists are trained to meet the demand.

Summary

- The treatment options in depression are medication, psychotherapy, combined medication and electroconvulsive therapy.
- Treatments for depression work, and the success rate in treating depression is as good as that in many other disease areas, both in terms of acute response to treatment and maintenance therapy.
- There is still a need for valid, reliable and high-quality, peer-reviewed clinical practice guidelines to help GPs make treatment decisions.
- Non-adherence with antidepressant medication is a major problem. Patients are more likely to stay on medication if they are given clear messages about the treatment and told what to expect.
- In acute depression, the response rate to effective psychological therapies is similar to that obtained with drugs. The more severe the depression, the less successful psychological therapy on its own is likely to be.
- People with severe depression usually need medication to alleviate vegetative symptoms. Psychological therapy may then be introduced to help them deal with day-to-day problems.
- Psychological therapies are effective when practised by appropriately trained therapists. Currently, there are insufficient numbers of therapists to meet the demand.

- Certain 'add-ons' from psychological models can be delivered in primary care and simple information, messages and booklets can be used to enhance the impact of drug treatment and to enhance coping skills.

- Until people who respond differentially to cognitive therapy or psychological therapy versus drugs can be identified, the choice of treatment will continue to depend on factors such as costs, the availability of therapists, or patient or clinician preference.

References

1   Keith S, Matthews SM. The value of psychiatric treatment: Its efficacy in severe mental disorders. *Psychopharmacol Bull* 1993; **29**: 427–31.

2   Materson BJ, Reda D, Cushman WC et al. Affairs Cooperative Study Group on Antihypertensive Agents. Single-drug therapy for hypertension in men: A comparison of six antihypertensive agents with placebo. *N Engl J Med* 1993; **328**: 914–21.

3   US Department of Health and Human Services. *Depression in Primary Care: Treatment Guidelines.* Rockville: Agency for Health Care Policy and Research, 1993.

4   Cornwall P, Scott J. The Treatment of Depression in Primary Care: Do the guidelines follow the guidelines on how to develop guidelines. Paper submitted for publication, 1998.

5   Lin EH, Von Korff M, Katon W et al. The role of the primary care physician in patients' adherence to antidepressant therapy. *Med Care* 1995; **33**(1): 67–74.

6   Katon W, Von Korff M, Lin E et al. Collaborative management to achieve treatment guidelines. Impact on depression in primary care. *JAMA* 1995; **273**(13): 1026–31.

7   Scott J. Editorial: Psychological treatments for depression — An update. *Br J Psychiatry* 1995; **167**: 289–92.

8   Sotsky S, Glass D, Shea T et al. Patient predictors of response to psychotherapy and pharmacotherapy: Findings in the NIMH treatment of depression collaborative research program. *Am J Psychiatry* 1991; **148**: 997–1008.

9   Hollon S, Shelton R, Davies D. Cognitive therapy for depression: conceptual issues and clinical efficacy. *J Cons and Clin Psychol* 1993; **58**: 352–9.

10 Scott A, Freeman C. Edinburgh primary care depression study: Treatment outcome, patient satisfaction and cost after 16 weeks. *BMJ* 1992; **304**: 883–7.

11 Evans M, Hollon S, DeRobeis R et al. Differential relapse following cognitive therapy and pharmacotherapy of depression. *Arch Gen Psychiatry* 1992; **49**: 802–8.

12 Scott C, Tacchi M, Jones R, Scott J. Abbreviated cognitive therapy for depression: A pilot study in primary care. *Behavioral Cognitive Psychother* 1994; **22**: 96–102.

The benefit of newer antidepressants versus tricyclic antidepressants

John Donoghue

This presentation focuses on the most commonly prescribed newer antidepressants, the selective serotonin re-uptake inhibitors (SSRIs), with emphasis on the generally accepted criteria for 'rational' prescribing. These key areas are examined from the perspective of primary care, where most depression is treated and the majority of antidepressant prescriptions are written.

The Department of Health uses four key criteria to define 'rational' prescribing: safety, effectiveness, appropriateness and economy. These criteria are widely used by groups such as Health Authority advisers and the National Prescribing Centre, and in publications including the *Effective Healthcare Bulletin*. Appropriateness and economy are difficult topics to discuss, and no controlled studies of clinical practice within the UK National Health Service have shown better cost-effectiveness for any single antidepressant or group of antidepressants over another, so these issues will not be discussed.

Several important safety issues are associated with antidepressants, all of which have been covered in the literature (Table I). Toxicity in overdose is an important consideration because the risk of suicide in people with depression is higher than that in the general population. Data for the antidepressants prescribed most often in the UK show that the number of deaths/million prescriptions in 1987–92 was 48 for dothiepin and 39 for amitriptyline [1]. This compares with less than five for the newer antidepressants paroxetine, lofepramine and fluoxetine. The tricyclic antidepressants (TCAs) dothiepin and amitriptyline, the most commonly prescribed

TABLE I   Safety issues associated with the use of antidepressants

- Toxicity in overdose
- Behavioural toxicity
- Cardiovascular effects
- Hepatotoxicity
- Other
— co-morbid physical illness
— co-prescribed medicines
— effect on seizure threshold
— distress from side-effects

agents in primary care in the UK for at least 20 years, are associated with a considerably greater risk of death from overdose than newer antidepressants.

Behavioural toxicity—sedation, anticholinergic cognitive impairment and postural hypotension—may occur in patients receiving TCAs. Many agents result in all of these symptoms, and the psychomotor impairment can affect quality of life and increase the risk of accidents. Behavioural toxicity is not a feature of the SSRIs.

The use of TCAs may also result in cardiotoxicity and hepatotoxicity, and complicate the treatment of co-morbid physical illness. These drugs may also have a pro-convulsive effect on seizure threshold. Other safety issues GPs need to be aware of when prescribing antidepressants are the effects of co-prescribed medicines and the distress caused to patients by unpleasant side-effects.

Data from clinical trials and meta-analyses of their results published over recent years show no differences in efficacy for any antidepressant or group of antidepressants over any other provided the drugs are prescribed at the minimum effective dose for an adequate period of time [2–4]. However, it is important to distinguish between effectiveness and efficacy. Efficacy is an indication of a drug's therapeutic potential, determined within the confines of a placebo-controlled, clinical trial. The patients are a highly selected group treated identically following a specific protocol, and the patient–doctor relationship differs from that found in the primary care setting. Both the practice of the doctors and the behaviour of the patients are constrained by the trial protocol. Efficacy is, therefore, a concept rather than an actuality. Effectiveness, on the other hand, concerns whether or not the drug delivers the desired outcome in real-world, clinical practice.

Outcome data on effectiveness are available from pragmatic and observational studies. The premise for looking at the effectiveness of antidepressants in clinical practice is that an adequate dose and duration of therapy is required for successful treatment [5]. Successful treatment is defined as the resolution of acute symptoms, return to normal functioning, prevention of relapse and control of healthcare costs. Literature on antidepressant outcomes and doses has been published for more than 25 years. Goethe *et al* compared treatment in 201 depressed patients discharged from psychiatric hospitals in the US, defining treatment intensity as 'probably inadequate' to 'probably adequate' and response from 'recovered' to 'unimproved' [6]. These authors were vague in their definitions because the study was retrospective, using case notes. They found that 36.3% of the patients had received 'probably inadequate' doses of antidepressants, even though they had attended specialist centres. A total of 28.8% of these patients recovered and 57.9% were unimproved, which is similar to the expected outcome with placebo in a clinical trial. Of the 45.3% who received 'probably adequate' doses, the reverse was true: 53.8% recovered and 24.6% were unimproved, this time similar to the expected result of active treatment in a clinical trial. The authors commented that "Differences in patient populations and outcome measures make it difficult to compare studies, but investigators have consistently demonstrated higher rates of response in patients given 'adequate' treatment" [6]. A consistent finding in the literature is that, as the intensity of antidepressant treatment increases, so does the outcome.

Frank et al carried out a series of studies looking at outcomes in recurrent depression. In a three-year follow-up of maintenance therapy with imipramine following recovery from an acute depressive episode, a 'full dose' of the drug (150–300 mg/day) was compared with a 'half dose' (75–150 mg/day) [7]. The survival rates (the mean time before the depression recurred) were 135 weeks on the full dose and 75 weeks on the half dose, which was described by the authors as "being no better than no antidepressant treatment". Despite this lack of effectiveness, the use of low doses of antidepressants has often been reported to be normal practice in primary care.

What constitutes an effective dose of antidepressant remains the subject of much debate. However, the literature on TCA dose is consistent: 125 mg/day should be regarded as the minimum effective dose for the treatment of major depression [8–13], although some GPs say their patients do well on lower doses. International guidelines, such as those published by the World Health Organization [14] corroborate this view.

Antidepressant use in the UK has been studied using a national medical records (DINLINK) database. The dataset included data from 100 practices across the UK, selected as a representative sample of UK primary care. This provided more than 750 000 patient records, representing more than 1% of the UK population. The database was scanned to identify prescriptions for antidepressants alongside which a diagnosis of depression was made by the GP and entered into the patient's notes. Prescriptions for anxiety, pain relief and other non-depression indications were excluded from the study.

Data obtained in this way have enabled the percentage of antidepressant prescriptions reaching an effective dose in the UK to be determined [15,16]. Only one patient in eight treated with the most commonly prescribed TCAs, amitriptyline, clomipramine and dothiepin, receive an effective dose at any time in their treatment. In contrast, approximately 80% of lofepramine treatments and 100% of SSRI prescriptions were at an effective dose. The Defeat Depression Campaign was underway at the time these prescribing patterns were observed and appears to have had no impact on the doses of TCAs given to patients.

Low-dose patterns of prescribing are seen in almost every country where studies have been conducted. In Denmark, Rosholm et al found average doses for TCAs were similar to those found in the UK, and that the only TCA used at an effective dose was clomipramine—and that was by psychiatrists, not GPs (Figure 1) [15]. Doses similar to those used in the UK were also found in Italy [16]. The Swedish Diagnosis and Therapy Survey of antidepressant prescribing also found that doses

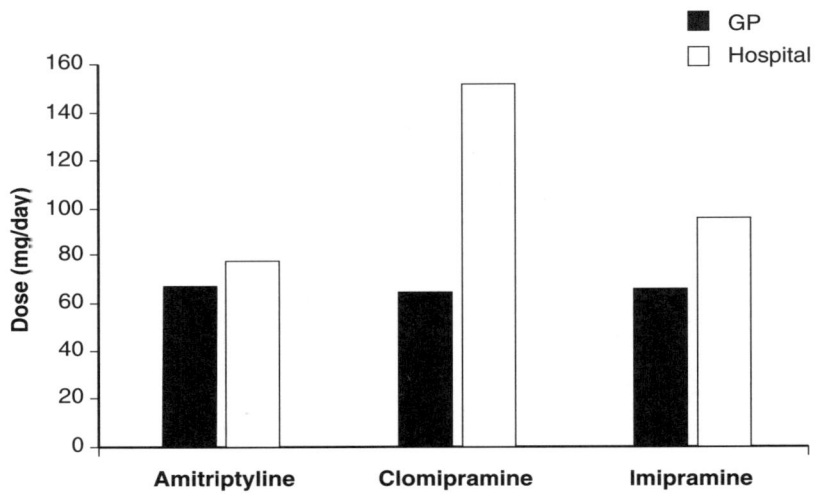

FIGURE I Doses of tricyclic antidepressants (TCAs) prescribed in Denmark. The only TCA used at an effective dose was clomipramine—and that was by psychiatrists, not GPs. Redrawn and reproduced with permission [15]

were low, and moreover found little evidence of dose titration with TCAs: the starting and final doses were 48 and 62 mg/day for amitriptyline and 50 and 70 mg/day for clomipramine, respectively [17].

Logistic regression analysis has recently been applied to antidepressant prescribing in primary care in the UK [18]. It has been used to determine the effect of the first antidepressant prescribed (by class) on subsequent patterns of treatment using data obtained on the most commonly prescribed antidepressants during the Defeat Depression Campaign. The main outcome measure indicates whether or not the patient has been prescribed an 'adequate treatment episode', demonstrating how prescribing compares with national guidelines for the treatment of depression. Unfortunately, the results are not yet published.

Few studies in the UK have examined the outcome of sub-optimal treatment. However, one study by Ali investigated 222 primary care patients in south Wales taking long-term, mainly low-dose, antidepressants [19]. 'Case-level' depression (ie depression that required an intervention of some kind) was found in 77% of these patients. Moderate-to-severe depression was present in 66% of patients. Those with moderate-to-severe depression consulted their GPs twice as often as age- and gender-matched controls. This indicates that ineffective treatment of depression increases the number of times a patient visits the surgery. Ali concluded that the "Continued use of subtherapeutic doses is ineffective and cannot be justified".

There are, therefore, clear distinctions between the older TCAs and the SSRIs in terms of safety. Although no difference in efficacy is reported, a difference in effectiveness is evident between the two classes. The equal efficacy suggested for these drugs from the results of randomized, placebo-controlled, trials is not delivered in clinical practice. This may explain why the outcomes of treating depression have remained consistently poor and why studies show that patients receiving antidepressants are reported to do no better than those who receive no therapy.

Summary

- 'Rational' prescribing is defined in terms of safety, effectiveness, appropriateness and economy.
- No controlled studies of clinical practice within the UK NHS have shown better cost-effectiveness for any single antidepressant, or group of antidepressants, over another.
- Clinical trials show no differences in efficacy for any antidepressant or group of antidepressants over any other, provided the drugs are prescribed at the minimum effective dose for an adequate period of time.
- In clinical practice, 30–80% of depressed patients with poor outcome are receiving inadequate doses of antidepressants, resulting in low treatment success rates.
- There are clear distinctions between the older TCAs and the SSRIs in terms of safety, with toxicity in overdose and other side-effects being more prevalent in the former. Behavioural toxicity is a feature of the TCAs but not the SSRIs.
- Patients who begin treatment with a TCA often remain on low doses, as dose titration seldom takes place.
- Although no difference in efficacy is reported between the TCAs and the SSRIs, a difference in effectiveness is evident between the two classes.
- The continued use of subtherapeutic doses of antidepressants is ineffective and cannot be justified.

References

1   Henry JA, Alexander CA, Sener EK. Relative mortality from overdose of antidepressants. BMJ 1995; **310**: 221–4.

2   Song F, Freemantle N, Sheldon T et al. Selective serotonin reuptake inhibitors: meta-analysis of efficacy and acceptability. BMJ 1993; **306**(6879): 683–7.

3   Montgomery SA, Henry J, McDonald G et al. Selective serotonin reuptake inhibitors: meta-analysis of discontinuation rates. Int Clin Psychopharmacol 1994; **9**: 47–53.

4   Anderson IM, Tomenson BM. The efficacy of selective serotonin reuptake inhibitors in depression: a meta-analysis of studies against tricyclic antidepressants. J Psychopharmacol 1994; **8**: 238–9.

5   Potter WZ, Rudorfer MV, Monji H. The pharmacologic treatment of depression. N Engl J Med 1991; **325**: 633–42.

6   Goethe JW, Szarek BL, Cook WL. A comparison of adequately vs. inadequately treated depressed patients. *J Nerv Ment Dis* 1988; **176**: 465–70.

7   Frank E, Kupfer DJ, Perel JM *et al*. Comparison of full-dose versus half-dose pharmacotherapy in the maintenance treatment of recurrent depression. *J Affect Disord* 1993; **27**: 139–45.

8   Paykel ES, Hollyman JA, Freeling P, Sedgwick P. Predictors of therapeutic benefit from amitriptyline in mild depression: a general practice placebo-controlled trial. *J Affect Disord* 1988; **14**: 83–95.

9   Thompson C, Thompson CM. Prescribing of antidepressants in general practice II: A placebo controlled trial of low dose dothiepin. *Human Psychopharmacol* 1989; **4**: 191–204.

10   Paykel ES, Priest RG. Recognition and management of depression in general practice: Consensus Statement. *BMJ* 1992; **305**: 1198–202.

11   Montgomery SA, Bebbington P, Cowen P *et al*. Guidelines for treating depressive illness with antidepressants: a statement from the British Association for Psychopharmacology. *J Psychopharmacol* 1993; **7**: 19–23.

12   Medicines Resource Centre. Selecting an antidepressant. *Medicines Resource Centre (MeReC) Bulletin* 1995; **6**(i): 1–4.

13   McPartlin GM. Drug choice in the treatment of depression? *Scot Med Res* 1997; **39**: 151–4.

14   WHO Mental Health Collaborating Centres. Pharmacotherapy of depressive disorders: a consensus statement. *J Affect Dis* 1989; **17**: 197–8.

15   Rosholm JU, Hallas J, Gram LF. Outpatient utilisation of antidepressants: a prescription database analysis. *J Affect Disord* 1993; **27**: 21–2.

16   Munizza C, Tibaldi G, Bollini P *et al*. Prescription pattern of antidepressants in out-patient psychiatric practice. *Psychol Med* 1995; **25**: 771–8.

17   Bingefors K, Isacson D, von Knorring L. Antidepressant dose patterns in Swedish clinical practice. *Int Clin Psychopharmacol* 1997; **12**(5): 283–90.

18   Donoghue J, Dunn RL, Ozminkowski RJ, Hylan TR. Longitudinal patterns of antidepressant prescribing in primary care in the United Kingdom. *J Psychopharmacol* 1999, in press.

19   Ali IM. Long-term treatment with antidepressants in primary care. *Psychiatric Bull* 1998; **22**: 15–19.

Antidepressant profile and diagnosis

Tim Bullock

Most cases of depression (97%) are treated in primary care, and 50% of cases remain undiagnosed. Only 40% of antidepressant prescriptions are for major depressive disorder, although the remaining 60% are for conditions that are often described as depression. The proportion of patients stopping treatment before four weeks have elapsed may be as high as 70% [1], and prescribed doses of tricyclic antidepressants (TCAs) are largely inadequate. There is, therefore, a need to address the issue of effective treatment in the primary care setting in order to improve the outcome for patients.

The DSM-IV classifies the main forms of depression as: major depressive disorder (MDD), dysthymia, recurrent brief depression, depression in obsessive–compulsive disorder, organic mood disorder and secondary depression. These are all different diseases, but primary care physicians, and even some psychiatrists, do not reliably recognize this range of conditions. Although depression can be divided up into categories other than MDD [2], most clinical trials of antidepressants focus on this condition—despite the fact that the clinical application of this drug class is, in reality, much wider. In patients with physical illness it is often difficult to decide whether a patient has an organic mood disorder or depression as a co-morbid reaction to their disease (ie secondary depression).

The lifetime treatment history of a depressed patient depends on their type of depression [2]. Double depression (MDD and dysthymia) has the greatest lifetime treatment history (80% of patients are treated at some time during their life), followed by combined depression (MDD and recurrent brief depression; 68%), dysthymia (50%), recurrent brief depression (48%) and MDD alone (36%). These results indicate that the conditions ostensibly treated in studies may bear closer scrutiny—particularly with respect to co-morbidity. People with depression tend to move between a number of different conditions (Figure 1) [2], so it is important that diagnoses other than MDD are considered and treated correctly.

In addition to the nature of the affective disorder(s), co-morbidity and differential diagnosis also need to be addressed by primary care doctors. Patients often present with co-morbid psychiatric illness (see page 5). The common differential diagnoses of depression are mixed anxiety–depression, obsessive–compulsive disorder, panic disorder, social phobia, generalized anxiety disorder and personality disorder. Many of these co-morbid and differentially diagnosed conditions are treated as uncomplicated MDD.

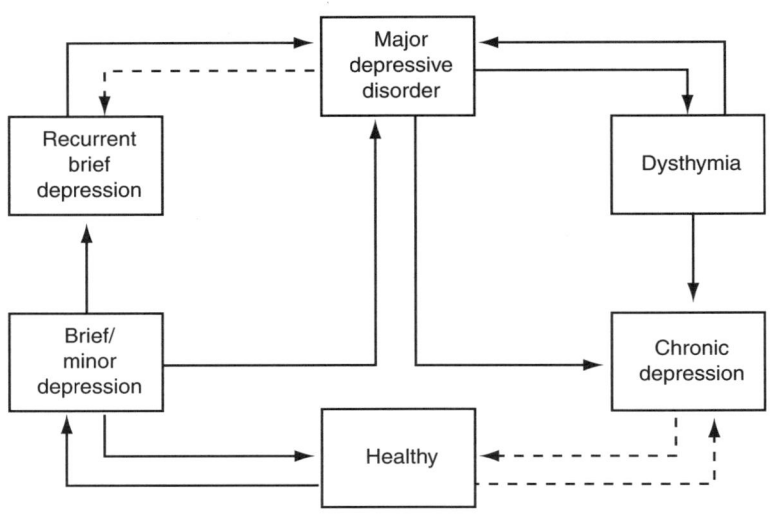

FIGURE I People with depression tend to move between a number of related disorders.
Redrawn and reproduced with permission [2]

The efficacy of certain antidepressants has been established in panic disorder and obsessive–compulsive disorder, for example. In panic disorder, serotonergic and non-serotonergic agents demonstrate different effects. For example the selective serotonin re-uptake inhibitor (SSRI), fluvoxamine, reduces the frequency of panic attacks and the mean Hamilton Anxiety Score more than the noradrenergic agent, maprotiline [3]. Similar differential effects have been reported in obsessive–compulsive disorder [4]. Although these conditions fall into the differential diagnosis for MDD, they do not have the same response to treatment.

People with brief recurrent depression do not respond to antidepressants. However, treatment with dopamine-blocking agents is effective: flupenthixol shows efficacy while the SSRIs and mianserin do not. There is, therefore, a spread of pharmacological response across the range of patients suffering depression, and these people do not form a diagnostically homogeneous group.

In order to optimize the treatment of depression, compliance and safety need to be considered, in addition to efficacy, across the range of indications. Compliance, or concordance, is a major issue that determines effectiveness and, therefore, outcome. Studies have shown that fewer patients taking SSRIs stop therapy compared with those receiving TCAs [5]. Treatment instruction—the way the clinician interacts with the patient in terms of achieving maximum concordance—forms a vital part of compliance. Treatment instruction has been poorly researched, but evidence suggests that it is related to the clinician's confidence in the medication. In order to prescribe properly and maximize compliance, doctors

TABLE I   Side-effects of the new antidepressants

Drug	Anti-cholinergic	Cardiac	Nausea	Sedation	Over-dose	Pro-convulsant	Sexual dysfunction	Discon-tinuation
Citalopram	0	±	++	0	0	0	+	+
Fluoxetine	0	0	++	0	0	0	+	±
Fluvoxamine	+	0	++	+	0	0		
Paroxetine	0	0	++	0	0	0	+	+
Sertraline	0	0	++	+	0	0	+	+
Mirtazepine	0	0	0	+	0	0	?	?
Nefazodone	+	0	++	+	?	?	0	+
Reboxetine	0	++	++	+	?	+	+	+

therefore need to have confidence in both the drug chosen and antidepressants *per se*.

The side-effects of the SSRIs (Table I) are broadly similar, and are fewer in number and severity than those of the TCAs. The other newer drugs, mirtazepine, nefazodone, reboxetine and venlafaxine, have different side-effect profiles which, overall, are similar to those of the SSRIs. According to Baldwin [6], it is impossible to compare the capacity of these drugs to generate sexual dysfunction because of variations in the way data are collected. 5-HT$_2$ antagonism appears to be beneficial in terms of sexual dysfunction (this is the case with nefazodone). However, sexual dysfunction is part of the depressive syndrome, and some paradoxical outcomes in terms of improvements have been reported for SSRIs, such as the beneficial effect on premature ejaculation. Although much has been made of sexual dysfunction, it is a relatively minor side-effect compared with others leading to non-compliance and patients seldom complain of it.

Treatment regimen has an impact on compliance, with once-a-day therapies having the greatest benefit. The half-lives of citalopram (33 h), fluoxetine (24–140 h; 168–216 h including its metabolite), fluvoxamine (13–22 h), paroxetine (24 h), sertraline (25–26 h), mirtazepine (20–40 h) and reboxetine (13 h) are appropriate for once-daily dosing. This is not the case for nefazodone (2–4 h) or venlafaxine (1–2 h), although a slow-release venlafaxine preparation is now available. Fluoxetine and its active metabolite norfluoxetine have long half-lives, giving the potential for adverse drug interactions. Sertraline and citalopram also have active metabolites.

If TCAs are superseded by these new antidepressants the GP is faced with the question of which agent to use as first-line therapy. To treat a patient successfully, the GP needs to convey accurate information about the drug of choice (treatment instruction). This may be difficult when there is an increasing range of new drugs

TABLE 2   Indications of the new antidepressants

Drug	Depression	Depression with anxiety	Panic with/out agoraphobia	Obsessive– compulsive disorder	Bulimia	Social phobia
Paroxetine	✓	✓	✓	✓		✓
Fluoxetine	✓	✓		✓	✓	
Fluvoxamine	✓			✓		
Sertraline	✓	✓				
Lofepramine	✓					
Mianserin	✓					
Citalopram	✓		✓			
Nefazodone	✓	✓				
Mirtazepine	✓					
Venlafaxine	✓					
Reboxetine	✓					

with dissimilar pharmacologies and ranges of side-effects. However, it is important that doctors give their patients accurate side-effect information; patients often tolerate side-effects if they are expected, but stop taking medication if they are not. Clinician familiarity with TCAs is probably an important factor in their continued use.

SSRIs have broad activity across many of the conditions treated under the general heading of 'depression', while noradrenergic drugs (mostly TCAs), and other agents with different pharmacologies, do not. This means that many people treated for differential diagnoses of MDD may be given ineffective treatment. This warrants further study in primary care, where the range of conditions treated under the general heading of depression is broadest; serotonergic drugs are efficacious in more of these 'primary care' conditions than other antidepressants. GPs' confidence in TCAs has yet to be eroded, despite their toxicity. Data on broad effectiveness and safety is important in this respect, as some GPs prescribe low doses of TCAs because of their sedative effects.

Continuing clinical education still has a long way to go and the Defeat Depression Campaign had little impact on prescribing behaviour. The promotion of new drugs, such as SSRIs, has increased the number of people receiving antidepressants overall, because prescriptions for TCAs have not declined concomitantly.

How can improvements be made? The safety of SSRIs compared with TCAs has been clearly demonstrated in terms of overdose, psychomotor impairment and drug interactions. The number of deaths/million prescriptions is under 10 for paroxetine, fluoxetine, fluvoxamine, sertraline, lofepramine and mianserin; 10–19 for clomipramine and trazodone; 20–39 for imipramine, phenelzine and maprotiline; more than 40 for amitriptyline, dothiepin and doxepine; and is currently unknown for nefazodone, mirtazepine, venlafaxine and reboxetine [7]. Caution should still be exercised when prescribing the very new antidepressants, as their efficacy across the range of indications is still to be established. Some evidence suggests that mirtazepine may be a good treatment for recurrent brief depression which is resistant to other therapies. There is no preferred treatment for all mood disorders and a range of different agents is still required. The area of drug interactions with SSRIs and other new agents has received much attention but, with few exceptions, the number of case reports of real toxicity is small. Specialist opinions are obviously needed for patients on complex regimens.

SSRIs have the broadest indications of the whole group of new antidepressants (Table 2). If this reflects proven efficacy, coverage of depression and its many faces in individual patients will also be broad. The other new drugs mostly have single indications, and from what is known of similar agents, they are unlikely to extend their indications as widely as the SSRIs.

In conclusion, consideration must be given to balancing the broad effectiveness of the antidepressants prescribed with their safety and tolerability. As the diagnosis of depression may be inexact in primary care, an agent with broad coverage is needed. The drug should cover a range of diagnostic possibilities. Practitioners' knowledge of and confidence in the agent of choice is highly important because compliance/concordance is such a significant issue.

Summary

- People with mood disorders may suffer from a number of different conditions, so it is important that diagnoses other than major depressive disorder are considered and treated correctly.
- Although many conditions are differential diagnoses for major depressive disorder, they do not respond in the same way to treatment.
- In order to prescribe properly and maximize compliance, doctors must have confidence in the disease areas, the drug chosen and antidepressants per se.
- To treat a patient successfully, GPs need to convey accurate information about the drug of choice (treatment instruction), which may be difficult when there is an increasing range of new drugs with dissimilar pharmacologies and ranges of side-effects.
- The side-effects of the SSRIs and other new antidepressants are broadly similar, and are fewer in number and severity than those of the TCAs.
- The safety of SSRIs, compared with TCAs, has been clearly demonstrated in terms of overdose, psychomotor impairment and drug interactions.

- Clinician familiarity with TCAs is probably an important factor in their continued use and GP confidence in these agents has yet to be eroded.
- We do not yet have the perfect treatment, so we currently need a range of different antidepressants.
- As the diagnosis of depression may be inexact in primary care, an agent with broad coverage is needed.
- SSRIs have the broadest indications of the whole group of new antidepressants. If this reflects proven effectiveness, coverage of depression and its many faces in individual patients will also be broad.

References

1   Johnson DAW. A Study of the use of antidepressant medication in general practice. *Br J Psych* 1974; **125**: 186–92.

2   Angst J. Course of mood disorders: A challenge to psychopharmacology. *Clin Neuropharmacol* 1992; **15**(1A): 444a–5a.

3   den Boer. *Serotonergic mechanisms in anxiety disorders; An inquiry into serotonin function in panic disorder.* Holland: ISBN 90-9002371-2.

4   Goodman WK, Price LH, Delgado PL *et al.* Specificity of serotonin reuptake inhibitors in the treatment of obsessive–compulsive disorder. Comparison of fluvoxamine and desipramine. *Arch Gen Psychiatry* 1990; **47**(6): 577–85.

5   Montgomery SA, Henry J, McDonald G *et al.* Selective serotonin reuptake inhibitors; meta-analysis of discontinuation rates. *Int Clin Psychopharmacol* 1994; **9**: 47–53.

6   Baldwin D, Thomas S. *Depression and sexual function.* 1997.

7   Henry JA, Alexander CA, Sener EK. Relative mortality from overdose of antidepressants. *BMJ* 1995; **310**(6974): 221–4.

The way forward

Malcolm Lader

From the presentations given today we have seen that depression is a series of complex overlapping conditions. It has many manifestations, making it difficult to diagnose in primary care. Although it can exist alone, it is often secondary to, or co-morbid with, a spectrum of different disorders, is common in all physical illness, and may have an organic cause.

Depression is underpresented by patients, under-recognized by GPs and under-treated, leading to poor outcome. Probably fewer than 50% of all depressed patients visit their GP, the most common reasons being perceived stigma, acceptance of depression (elderly people), poor expectations of treatment and beliefs that doctors are unsympathetic. Primary care doctors often misdiagnose depression as anxiety or mixed anxiety and depression, and 50% of all cases of depression go unrecognized. Many GPs feel that they do not understand enough about depression to make the diagnosis and initiate the right treatment. They also believe they have neither the time nor the skills to deal with what happens next if they diagnose depression, and are unaware that depressed people are potentially rewarding to treat. There is a fundamental ambivalence to drug treatment in both doctors and patients and GPs may be prescribing antidepressants in a half-hearted fashion, believing they are not warranted in the same way as antibiotics.

In addition, some health authorities give out the message that too much depression, with its associated costs, is being diagnosed. Time constraints (or perceived time constraints) during consultations often result in the treatment of physical symptoms, rather than the underlying problem in somatizing depressed patients. Undiagnosed and unmanaged depression has important time and cost implications, as the patient inevitably returns to the surgery for further consultations.

The treatment options for depression in primary care are medication, psychotherapy, or combined medication and psychotherapy—with the choice dependent on costs, the availability of therapists or patient or clinician preference. Contrary to misconception, treatments for depression are effective, and the treatment success rate is as good as that in many other disease areas, both in terms of acute response to treatment and maintenance therapy. However, adherence to anti-depressant medication is a major problem. The reasons for this may be inadequate patient instruction by the GP, a lack of information for both GP and patient as to what to expect (eg in terms of side-effects) and a lack of perceived benefit on the part of both patients and doctors. Antidepressant treatment is often inadequate in terms of both dose (see below) and length of therapy. The duration of

Clear take-home messages about depression for GPs

General
- Depression is a chronic or relapsing disease.
- Most episodes of depression are self-limiting and resolve over time. Treatment will support the patients until they get well again. Without treatment the depression may worsen, with potentially negative consequences for the patient.
- The management of depression needs to change, and improved intra- and inter-College networking is needed in this respect. PRIMHE, for example, has recently been set up to promote the positive aspects of depression management. Non-medical practice staff do have an important role to play.

Diagnosis
- Watch out for groups at particular risk of developing depression: such as elderly people, individuals with co-morbid physical illnesses and those who have suffered bereavement or redundancy.
- Depression in elderly people is common, yet they tend to accept it and seldom report their mood. Watch out for recent changes in health, circumstances and consulting behaviour in this patient group.
- Ask about functional behavioural changes (eg ability to handle money) as these may indicate depression.
- Always consider depression in patients who report insomnia of recent onset.
- When patients present with mixed symptoms, anxiety is easy to spot. Look beyond the anxiety for signs of depression (eg loss of libido, sleep and appetite).
- Do not make a primary diagnosis of anxiety unless depression has been excluded.
- Patients who often return to the surgery with physical symptoms may be somatizing; look beyond this for signs of depression.
- If you suspect depression, ask the patient what they think might have brought on their symptoms and if there is a chance they might be depressed.
- As the symptoms of depression are sometimes complex and diagnosis may be difficult, monitor and review the diagnosis periodically, changing therapy if required.
- Be sympathetic to patients with depression, so that they are encouraged to visit you.

(Continued)

Clear take-home messages about depression for GPs

Treatment

- In the confusion presented by the many symptoms of depression it may be difficult to find the aetiology of the disease, but treat it anyway (first aid).
- Antidepressants do work, but they must be taken at the correct dose (inadequate doses of TCA are still being given) and for the right length of time. Stress this to patients.
- Newer antidepressants, such as the SSRIs, not only have fewer side-effects than the TCAs, but are more effective (NB real-world effectiveness is often better than clinical-trial efficacy).
- Antidepressants with proven efficacy in anxiety disorders may be preferable.
- To maximize compliance give the patient clear messages about the treatment and what to expect: 'take the antidepressant daily'; 'the drug must be taken for 2–4 weeks for a benefit to be seen'; 'continue taking the medication even if you feel better'; and 'do not stop taking it without consulting me'. Also give instructions as to how to resolve specific problems—for example, what to do about missed doses—and tell patients which side-effects they are likely to experience.
- If a patient is trying alternative medicine, and there is no likelihood of adverse interaction, suggest their conventional agent is taken at the same time.
- Simple information, messages and booklets can be used to enhance the impact of drug treatment and to encourage compliance by allowing greater patient empowerment.

antidepressant treatment averages just six to nine weeks in the UK, while six months of medication is recommended.

No controlled studies of clinical practice in the UK NHS have shown better cost-effectiveness for any single antidepressant or group of antidepressants over another. The efficacies of these agents have also been shown to be similar in clinical trials. However, in clinical practice, many patients receive inadequate doses of tricyclic antidepressants (TCA), resulting in low treatment success rates. In addition, GPs are still prescribing low doses of TCAs, with their unpleasant side-effects and requirement for dose titration, when well-tolerated, easy-to-use alternatives, such as the selective serotonin re-uptake inhibitors (SSRIs) and other new drugs, are available for treating the many symptoms of this condition. The reasons for this are unclear, but may relate to familiarity, fear of change, beliefs that patients will not tolerate higher doses and confusion between sedation and anxiety reduction. This is despite evidence that a much higher proportion of SSRI prescriptions reach known effective doses than those for TCAs. Although TCAs and SSRIs have similar efficacies, there is a clear difference in effectiveness between the two classes.

Antidepressant treatment needs to cover a broad spectrum of conditions, as not all medications address every facet of depressive illness and a diagnosis of depression may not be exact in primary care. SSRIs have the broadest indications of the whole group of new antidepressants. If this reflects proven effectiveness, coverage of depression and its many faces in individual patients will also be broad.

What can be done to improve the outcome for patients with depression? There is a great need for education in order to change the perceptions and attitudes of both healthcare professionals and the public. Although the Defeat Depression Campaign brought some aspects of depression to attention, it has had little effect on prescribing practice and perceived stigma. Further campaigns and patient support groups are needed to encourage people to go to their doctor and say they are depressed. Without clear, accurate, patient education to inform people that anti-depressants work and that non-addictive agents with minimal side-effects are available, compliance will always be a problem. Patients with depression are entitled to the same level of service and treatment as those in other medical specialties, and only by becoming vocal will their needs be recognized. The role of patient user groups is pivotal in supporting patients and GPs alike.

The education of doctors in mental health needs to be improved at all stages, from medical school through to postgraduate education. It is essential that GPs are persuaded to change their prescribing practice so their patients receive the most effective and well-tolerated medication at the correct dose for a sufficient length of time. It will be difficult to educate all GPs without a great deal of time and effort, so in the meantime they can be given clear take-home messages to bear in mind during consultations (see table).

Although depression and mental illness are low on the list of priorities in terms of resources and education, mental health has been designated a priority area by the Government. Major opportunities exist within the setting of primary care groups for everyone to be involved in putting important messages across. Today, we identi-fied that improving the outcome for patients with depression was a 'management of change' issue, and that the change should be effected by healthcare professionals working together at all levels.

Non-medical staff within the practice can play an important part in this change. We have seen that nurse prescribing of SSRIs has encouraging results, with the effect that practice nurses now believe in antidepressants, see them working and recognize them as part of a range of treatments. The nurses will disseminate this information to their colleagues and, in turn, to patients. Health visitors, practice nurses and midwives can be taught to carry out assessments, perhaps using depres-sion scales, to 'filter out' patients with depression. By having a high index of suspicion, even community pharmacists can become involved in effecting change by suggesting a customer visits their GP.

Conclusion

Depression is a multifaceted condition, but this should not prevent the medical profession from putting its best effort into its detection. The correct diagnosis of depression may be provided by both recognizing and having a deeper understanding of the complexity of the disease. Correct diagnosis will lead to appropriate treatment and this, in turn, will save time and costs, and alleviate much human misery.